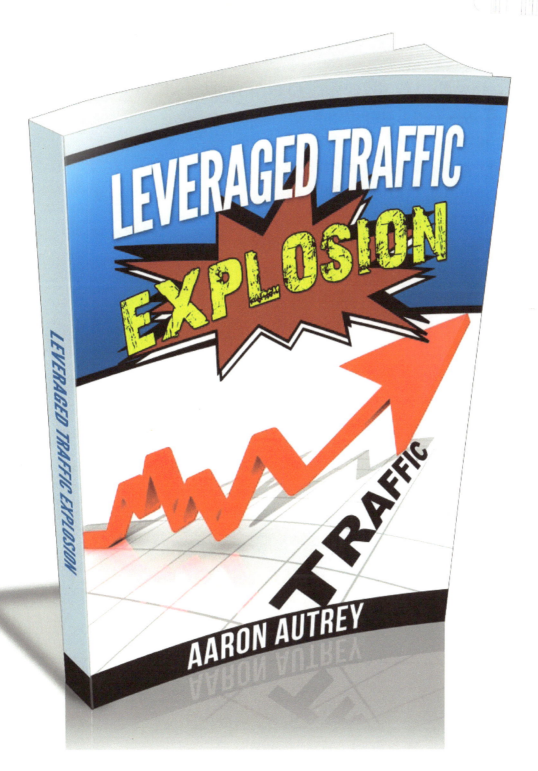

TABLE OF CONTENTS

Preface - Welcome!

Hello folks! Aaron Autrey here···

They call me the Network Marketing / Online Entrepreneur Dude. I tend to title all my products with the end word of "Frenzy" because that's what marketing is all about, creating a frenzy··· an excitement in others to take action. I'm ready to knock your socks off and teach you how to get over 1,000 leads in 14 days or less with Mini JV Giveaway Events.

Easier said than done? Nahh··· it's actually pretty simple.

When I first started in network marketing I would have killed for something like this and I'm so glad it was found and am glad to share it with you all.

This information can and will actually CHANGE YOUR LIFE if you allow it to. What good can you do with 1,000 extra leads, subscribers, sales, etc in the next 10-14 days? A lot right?

What if you sit there and don't take action? Then absolutely NOTHING IN YOUR LIFE WILL CHANGE, and you better believe that.

I went through this a while back and have realized putting in your due diligence will absolutely make this worth your while and you will certainly see a positive change in your income.

Without any further adieu, let's keep reading!

First, let's have an overview of the product.

OVERVIEW

This product, as mentioned in the Table of Contents on Page 2, is going to cover a number of things about a Mini JV Giveaway Event.

The main things we'll go over are:

1) How JV Giveaway Events work
2) The Tools you'll need
3) How to set it all up
4) How to find contributors
5) Sending traffic to it
6) Monetizing your incoming traffic
7) How you'll be the biggest winner of 'em all!
8) Participating in the JV events and some tips for success

BUT··· wait···

Let's pause for a moment···

I just want to say something···

It's really important you take this info in and read this product multiple times. Reason being is this product is going to be different and better than what you've seen.

Things really CAN CHANGE for you if you apply the knowledge you have here and take it to the moon. At least shoot for the stars and reach the moon, if you know what I mean.

*** If you read anything in this product, read this page please! ***

Matt Bacak put together one of the most successful JV Giveaway Events ever not too long ago.

And guess what?

He readily admitted *something insane in a video / conference* regarding the event:

"I didn't know what I was doing, I just went forward and worried about the little stuff as it came to me." (I'm paraphrasing)

****

Guys, LISTEN.

If you let yourself get in the way of yourself, you **_won't get anywhere online,_** **including JV events. Please get out of your own way and be successful.**

Stop using excuses or asking silly questions and just do the damn thing.

Worrying about "where I'm gonna find contributors" and "will I get enough contributors" and all this other stuff is rubbish⋯ Start it, market it (we give plenty of tips) and complete it. Just do it⋯

Thank you guys for reading the most important page of this book!

Module 1: How Mini JV Giveaway Events work

"JV" stands for Joint Venture.

A Joint Venture is when 2 or more marketers get together to do something that pools each others resources together to accomplish a specific task. In our case of course it's <u>Traffic.</u> Which leads to subscribers / leads, then which leads to sales, which leads to us profiting and making those $$.

<u>What is a Giveaway event?</u>

A "Mini JV Giveaway Event" is a group of marketers who usually know each other online or by acquaintance to join together to trade traffic, give away free products, and gain subscribers and eventually sales.

We use a website and a script to do so, but I'll show you how you can do this without having to install a long, horrendous script and save you tons of time!

Anyhow, each marketer tells their list about the event and they go onto the website, sign up (you collect their email of course), download free gifts and buy whatever it is the marketers are selling.

It's a win / win / win for all!

The contributors win by getting new subscribers and making some sales, the consumers of course win because they get free gifts, and the host of the event wins because he gets the most subscribers.

How does the host win?

The host of the event gets ALL of the subscribers for the entire event!

This is where you come in!

Can you imagine finding just 10 marketers who send 100 a piece (Super easy to send 100), and boom there is 1,000 fresh, new subscribers waiting to hear from you via email! Think of finding 50-100 marketers! I teach you ways to do this and how to market the event almost effortlessly below, so keep reading!

Typically events last 14 days. It really depends on what you as the host want to do! It's your event! Go for it!

Check out my proof below:

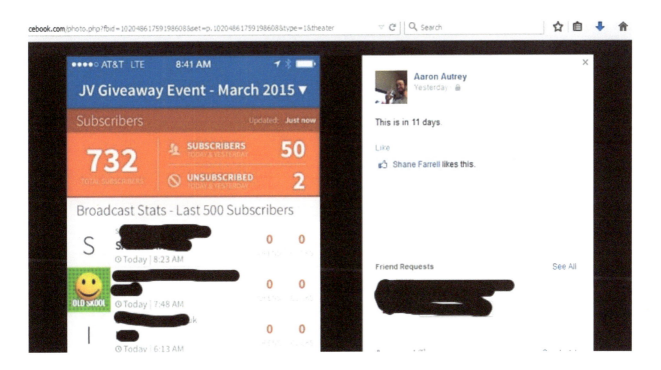

And it wasn't even done yet!

Paid membership vs Free membership

This comes down to personal preference.

You can either have your contributors pay $10-20 to join up because they know they're going to get a ton of subscribers for their list. Also, you can run a cash contest and have top 3-5 places paid out.

So, for example the 1st place person (who gets most members to sign up) gets $100, then the 2nd gets $50, then the 3rd gets $25. $175 in prize money and you found 20 contributors at $10 a piece··· You've gained $25 but also had some GREAT incentive for people to join up.

I prefer free membership, because honestly it's the only type of JV event that I've done and I've been successful with them.

Homework

- Read through again to be sure you understand it.
- Do you want to do a paid event or free one?
- Move onto the next module

Module 2: Tools you'll Need

Hosting

Hosting allows others to view your website or webpage, in this case will be the squeeze pages.

I love Hostgator and use them often, www.hostgator.com

Autoresponder - Aweber

I use Aweber all the time and their delivery rate is amazing and very fast. They are the best auto responder in my opinion. www.aweber.com

Click Magick - Link Tracking

Tracking your links is important but not absolutely necessary to having a successful Mini JV Event.

Really the only reason you would want to track links is to actually track the clicks from your broadcasts you send out to your email list to tell people about the event. Or if you place a link on Facebook or Twitter groups, and you want to track the clicks. That's always fun to do.

www.clickmagick.com or Click Magick, it's only $17 a month for 10,000 clicks tracked.

Installing a Script

If you're like me you want this to be as easy and quick as possible to start and setup your Mini JV Giveaway event.

Installing a script is easy, NO CODING REQUIRED!···.. Its only $8.50
http://jvgiveawayplugin.com/

Cheap Domains

You can visit 1and1.com to buy super cheap domains, you only need one :-)
They start at 99 cents and go up from there depending on what you want.

I buy from GoDaddy.com only because I've had such a long relationship with
them.

Homework

- Buy a domain
- Get Hosting
- Get Aweber
- Track your clicks (optional) with Click magick
- Move onto the next module

Module 3: Setting it All Up

With The JV Giveaway Plugin by Kevin Fahey, you can buy it, install it and have complete control over the entire thing. Very easy⋯ B uy it here f or $8.50 of if you want m ultiple sites it's only $13.50! jvgiveawayplugin.com/

Checklist

1) Buy a domain
2) Install the plugin
3) Follow the videos and do exactly as he says.

Wanna watch my setup video?

You may find it easier to watch. Visit here FOR IT. http://risewithaaron.com/installwp/installwp.htm

TIP: Remember not to delete any "Posts" and "Pages", just add one Page called "giveaway".

Below is what you'll see as the Affiliate Options and how to setup your page. It really doesn't take long at all. Follow the instructions.

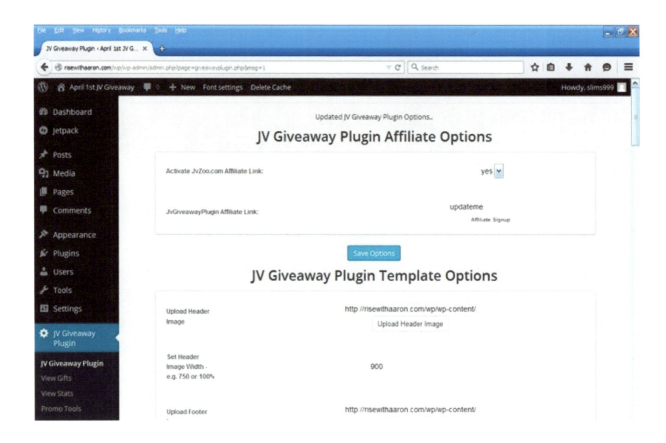

Also see what your page will actually look like below:

This is an example of what your page will look like. Remember, you get 10 different theme options, the Ninja is just 1 of 10.

Installing Plugin Tip

1) Do NOT remove any posts or pages from the beginning. Just simply add a page and call it "giveaway". Then start your installation process.

Homework

- Copy exactly what I do in the video
- Move onto the next module

Module 4: Finding Contributors

You're all set up now! How do we get this started? How do we get traffic?

Finding contributors to send you traffic is much easier than you may be thinking it is right now··· I'm sure you know at least 5-10 marketers online right now that would love to have a bunch of new, fresh subscribers added to their list over the next 2-4 weeks, right? If not you can find them···

Boosting Facebook Posts

This is the only way I'm going to show you that may *cost a little bit of dough*··· **all the other ways are free.**

Boosting Facebook Posts is a great way to get the word out there. It does cost a minimum of $20 but your post is already targeted to only those you want to see it.

Typically you can only Boost Facebook Posts from a Facebook page you have created. You don't want to boost a post from your own Facebook page, but I mean a Facebook PAGE for yourself, such as a Public Figure page.

Go to Facebook.com and find Create Page:

Public Figure:

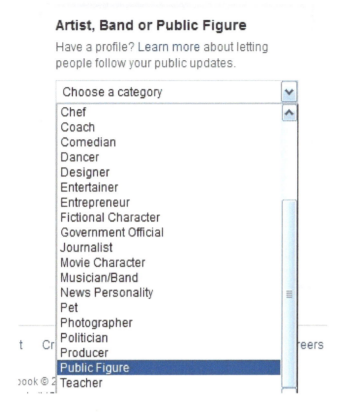

Answer the 4 main questions:

Remember that on #4 - Preferred Page Audience

You'll want to narrow down your audience using these particular audiences (that I use for my page). I use 4 of them, and you can add and change them later.

I use:

"internet marketing"
"online marketing"
"affiliate marketing"
"self employed and loving it"

Start with those 4, you'll have at least 500,000 - 1,000,000 audience members instead of 30-50,000,000 plus. That's way too many. We want to find people who are already in marketing.

YOUR PUBLIC FIGURE PAGE IS CREATED! Now you can boost posts!

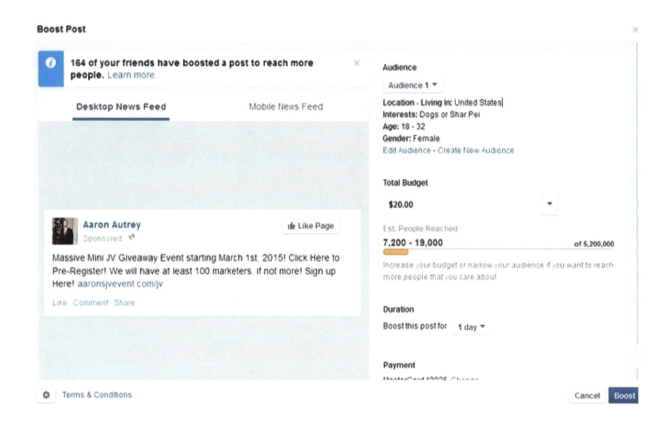

$20 gets me 7,200 - 19,000 people, especially if people like this and share it, etc etc.

Excellent!

Let's go over another way to find contributors!

Warriorforum.com Joint Ventures Section

Go to warriorforum.com and scroll down to find this section

Warrior Joint Ventures (33 Viewing)
Looking for a joint venture or partners? Tens of millions of dollars have been made through partnerships established through Warrior Joint Ventures.

Looking for writers
by rohitdhawan20
15th February 2

Inside you will find tons of people wanting to market with you.

Create a post with a title "Mini JV Giveaway Event starting _____ 1st, 2015" or whatever date you wish. Usually 5-10 days out is good enough.

In the body of the post you can put something like:

"Hey guys! I'm starting a Mini JV Giveaway event starting on (date) and am needing some contributors to join up! All you have to do is sign up, give away a free product, and watch the traffic roll in! Get as many sign ups as you can because the more you get, the more traffic you'll get. Looking forward to see you, PM me with any questions."

And boom! You've just used the largest internet marketing forum on the internet to boost your Mini JV Giveaway Event!

Easy right?

Facebook Groups

This section is pretty self-explanatory, but I'll go over it.

The Facebook group I use is Epic JV. Check it out
https://www.facebook.com/groups/epicjv/
All you do is post what I wrote above into the event and you should find a couple of contributors there who can send you traffic as well.

Here are a few more groups to join and post on:

https://www.facebook.com/groups/342070355912454/

https://www.facebook.com/groups/357671671043863/
https://www.facebook.com/groups/soloadexpert/

JV Giveaway Websites

My favorite and the one I'm participating in as I'm writing this is StarJV.com Visit http://www.starjv.com/event/ to check it out.

On these websites you can join up as a contributor to these people hosting the event right away, start sending traffic and making sales!

I signed up, sent an email out and got a quick $6 sale today within 20 mins of sending the broadcasts to one of my lists which is only 800 people. 4 people joined and I had 1 sale that quick.

They even provide email swipes (titles and body) to send to your subscribers!

You can also try these sites

New JV Giveaways
JV Giveaway Events Updater
JV Giveaway Blog

Homework

- Make a Facebook page and test a few post boosts!
- Use the Warrior Forum often as I mentioned
- Read and participate in 3 Facebook Groups
- Read and learn from those JV Giveaway Sites I mentioned
- Move onto the next module

Module 5: Sending Traffic

So!

You found 5-10 partners / contributors (minimum) and you have your site and everything ready. Now you begin, but need to contribute a little right? Therefore you need to send some traffic.

Obviously you don't really need to send a ton but you want to send some so that the host (you) doesn't look like a slouch and it gets things started right away.

You're getting your contributors EXCITED about joining your JV because··· you sent traffic! Hey this host rocks! He's sending us traffic just for joining··· exactly.

Obvious Side Note: Also remember this method isn't just for you obviously. It's for your contributors too right?

So remind them they need to be sending traffic and tell them to use these methods I'm about to show you.

The more they send the higher up the leaderboard they will be, which means the more traffic they will get!

Sending Broadcasts

PLEASE READ FIRST: *Sending Broadcasts only works if you have a list of people. As you read further in **this section only**, I will talking like I just started, because when I started out I only had around 500-700 people on my list at the* *time and I'll speak about the results I got then. If you have way more than that, then multiply and see what your potential is. If you don't know how to build a list, learn how at the warrior forum.*

Sending broadcasts is my favorite and the easiest, especially if you have a decent sized list. When I first started out I got 500 subscribers within 20 days, then rapidly got to 50-150 a day.

When I started and would send broadcasts I would get 8-10% open rates and 1-2% clicks. Now it's almost double that.

Let's say starting out you have 500 subs, you should get 5-12 clicks and 2-4 joins (free). It doesn't seem like much does it?

What if you have 5,000 subscribers, in one week you've sent 150-300 clicks to help out your cause.

Each of your contributors has 1,000 - 10,000 and they send 1 broadcast a day to your Mini JV Giveaway Event page··· Wowzzaaa!! Tons of traffic and EVERY SINGLE ONE OF THOSE OPT-INS GOES TO YOU!

POTENTIAL POTENTIAL POTENTIAL POTENTIAL :-)

Click Banking or Buying Funnel Clicks

Anybody can start doing this right away, even as a newbie.

Click banking is when you're building a list quickly and have bonus links to other people's squeeze pages and give them traffic.

You made a deal with them before hand to send a certain number of "clicks" or hits and they will in-turn send them back to you.

So you have traffic sent to YOUR SQUEEZE PAGE > YOUR BONUS PAGE which has your click banking partners links on it, so you send them traffic.

Once you send the appropriate number of clicks you agreed upon, they send them back to you.

Since I've been click banking, I'd sometimes have as many as 200-500 clicks coming into my banking funnel per day, which in turn sends traffic to my partners.

Now guess what, they owe me traffic and boom there goes the cycle over and over.

You grow your list SUPER RAPIDLY at this point when you're doing 100-500+ clicks per day.

What does click banking have to do with sending traffic. Will for a day or two, depending on how much traffic you're getting, you can send some traffic to the Mini JV Giveaway Event page and get some sign ups, sales, etc etc.

Banking is similar to the Giveaway Event, in which you're trading traffic.

When you start click banking, you can buy what we call "funnel clicks". Funnel clicks are actually cheaper and a little "better" than solo ads, which is what we're going to talk about next.

The only downfall to funnel clicks is that it may take a lot longer for people to send funnel clicks. Solo ads are typically 1-2 days total to receive. Funnel clicks are sometimes 7-14 days!

Here are some Facebook groups to easily find people to buy from:

https://www.facebook.com/groups/1462801947294857/
https://www.facebook.com/groups/funnelclicks/

<u>Buying Solo Ads</u>

Anybody can do this method easily even if you're a newbie

You can go to some Facebook Groups to find quality solo vendors (by reading their testimonials) who you see lots of people trust and buy a solo ad from them.

You can have them send the traffic (clicks) to the affiliate link, or send them to your squeeze page which then has a bonus page with your affiliate link on it.

Solo ads range from 40-65 cents per click. They are better in that they can usually get traffic to you within 1-2 days but aren't quite as strong as funnel clicks.

Funnel clicks are already going through a funnel, so they're clicking away. Solo ads are from people's email list, therefore they are not quite as in a clicking frenzy. But this is still quality, especially if you find a good vendor, and there are a ton of good vendors out there.

You can find solo ad vendors in these groups.

https://www.facebook.com/groups/SoloAdsTestimonials/?ref=br_tf
https://www.facebook.com/groups/salestestimonials/
https://www.facebook.com/groups/soloads/

These 3 groups will keep you going.

****

Understand that the last 2 methods, *click banking* and *buying solo ads* are extremely similar.

A solo ad will get your 100-1000+ clicks to your JV page where members can sign up for free gifts.

Clickbanking is when you're trading traffic with partners and after you get traffic back from them, the traffic will receive an email via Aweber. As a welcome email you can add the link to your JV event. It works well with signing up members.

Homework

- Build a list and use broadcast emails
- Use clickbanking to send traffic to your offers
- Use solo ads to send traffic to your offers
- Move onto the next module

Module 6: Monetize the Traffic for $$

CPA - Clicksure and Cash Network

CPA = Cost Per Action

This basically means that all this incoming traffic you have needs to go somewhere right? Well it's obviously going to go to your Aweber account and you'll fill up your subscriber base.

But don't we need to see some income? Of course!

All of the traffic that comes through we're going to want to filter it to a certain CPA offer or "make money online" offer I'll show you in the next sections. CPA is great though because the companies have good, converting offers and they pay pretty well.

The only downfall to CPA is sometimes you have to wait 32 days to get your check, sometimes just 4 days.

Go to www.clicksure.com to sign up for Click Sure. Go to www.cashnetwork.com to sign up for Cash Network.

Here's an example of a CPA offer = Larry's Cash Machine

As you can see, if you log into your clicksure.com account (today as of Feb 18th, 2015 as I'm writing this) you'll see Larry's Cash Machine at the top. It's the Number 1 offer at Clicksure right now.

So you click on it and see this:

It's a great offer because A) it's number 1, B) the sales page looks great (sign in and check it out yourself), but ya know what? It's a $200 payout and it's a Weekly Net 32. So if you want your subscribers to be taken to a more expensive offer you can, but I don't recommend it because they don't convert as well. Plus, it's going to take 32 days to get paid.

So let's check another one⋯

My Online Business

This one pays out in almost half the time, and as you can see "Pays a crazy $120 on a $49 sale!!"

Therefore you can choose this one if you like.

Hey, choose what you want!

But you might as well send these (freebie seekers) to a lesser paying offer because you'll get more sales and you'll get paid almost twice as fast.

$1 Products

You can make a killing sending your traffic to lower paying offers, especially $1 offers that over-deliver. Can you imagine buying a $30 product for $1?

How does that feel to you? Whoever just sold it to you is CRAZY and really over-delivers and really cares about your success obviously.

He wanted you to have it so bad that he changed it from $30 to $1.

Well that's how most people feel about high-quality $1 products! They are a steal and people buy them left and right.

How do you find them?

I have several places.

You can check out Branden Pierce's MRR rights to his $1 product. I bought it for $17 and use it all the time.

MRR (Master Resell Rights) Rights means you can sell his product for at least $1 or more. I keep it at $1.

Check it out
http://brandenpierce.com/products/easy-buyer-profits/oto2/

Other Ways to Monetize

Your Own Products

You can use your own products of course if you have them. The best reason to use your own products is because they come from YOU and you make 100% commission.

You have complete control of your own products as well and can edit and do with them as you see fit.

ClickBank.com

You can also send them to a Click Bank product that obviously has to do with "make money online" and you will make some good money doing that.

I say that because there are some pretty brilliant products on Click Bank, and they work kind of like big CPA offers.

PPL - Pay Per Lead

I talked about PPL and how I love it back in my first product I ever made, Freebie List Frenzy--> http://www.warriorforum.com/warrior-special-offers/1044976-gain-massive-amounts-subscribers-discover-easy-follow-steps-effectively-monetize-list.html

PPL is simple. A favorite of mine I'm using right now is James Jordan's Cash Superstar PPL program. Google it for details and to sign up.

PPL is highly recommended by not only by myself but I know many other marketers who use it and make money daily.

Homework

- Apply for at least 2 CPA networks
- Use $1 products or your own products if you have them
- Sign up for Clickbank.com and use their products
- Sign up with a couple of PPL programs and use them
- Move onto the next module

Module 7: The Do's and Dont's of Hosting an Event

Do's

- Invite as many contributors as humanly possible
- Send a MINIMUM of 200 clicks and get some members, it should really be way more
- Be patient with your contributors and contact them on a regular basis
- Monetize your incoming traffic
- Use Facebook
- Use Special Offers section to sell $7-27 products, even some are $97
- Have a support email out there
- Important: Send a thank you email for joining
- Believe it'll work!!! Because it will!

Dont's

- Send bad traffic to help your contributors, they want to see you care
- Be impatient
- Be too lazy with this, it takes a little work and organization
- Invite family and friends :-) Just use marketers
- Be unprofessional

Homework

- Keep the Do's and Dont's in mind at all times, refer back to this if needed
- Move onto the next module

Module 8: End Results

Who's the big winner? We talked about it before…

You are!

Why??

You end up getting everyone's subscriber when you host a Mini JV Giveaway Event!

Invite just 10 people, let's say 6 of them participate. 6 of them send in 100 people (sign ups), that's easy math right? You're at 600 subs. What if they have decent sized lists? You're at well over 1,000 subs.

What if you found 10-20 people to contribute all at different ranges and sizes of list? You can see the potential right?

You've done what exactly?

You've paid $40 to setup your entire event
You've spoke to 10-20 people and found 5-10 of them to contribute.
You've gained hundreds, if not thousands of subscribers through the 14 day process and made plenty of dough!

Sounds good to me!

Homework

- Understand this module
- Move onto the next module

Module 9: Sticking Points

Where will you get stuck?

Question) It's too hard to install this!

Answer) If the videos don't help you (which they should) then email me at aaronautrey9.ru and I can help. The videos make it very easy though.

Honestly, you should really visit http://aaronautrey.com/leveraged/lteoto.html because it's way faster··· It's my One-Time-Offer to you, but I'm giving it away for $9!

Question) How long do I run it??

Answer) No longer than 14 days. There's no need, just start a new one!

Question) I only found 2 contributors, is that enough?

Not quite··· You'll need at least 5-10 contributors, preferably 10 to make it worth your while. Hey if you want to do 2-3 that's fine to start out and you can have fun with it! Try it out!

Nothing wrong with that.

But eventually you'll want to go big.

How to find contributors...

Have you joined a coaching program?
Are people on warriorforum.com familiar with you?
Have you posted in warriorforum.com like I showed you?
Have you done MLM's or email marketing before?
Are you in any type of marketing groups on Facebook?

If not, and you don't have a base, or group of marketing friends you can still find them. You can find them in marketing groups on Facebook or you can find people on warriorforum.com in the [Warrior Joint Ventures](#).

Homework

- Understand this module
- HAVE FAITH!! YOU CAN DO THIS!!
- Move onto the next module

Module 10: Aaron being Aaron for a second...

We are now at the end of this guide and I want you to hear something...

What are you doing right now to get better at life? Financially, emotionally, physically?

Are you doing nothing or are you reading this guide and ready to take action?

What will happen if you don't do this? I CAN TELL YOU!

YOU WON'T FRIGGEN GET ANYWHERE!

I hate when people complain and moan about "It's not God's time for me" - "It's not the universes time for me"...

SCREW THAT!

If you want to be in the same place as you are today in 2 weeks from now, fine then don't do anything. But if it were me, I would take this guide and run with it and see how far you can go!

Where would Aaron (3rd person) be if he kept going to school and racking up student loan debt for a music degree?

HE WOULD BE A POOR, BROKE DRUMMER (I love to drum) ON THE SIDE OF THE ROAD BANGING TRASH BAGS FOR PENNIES!

Don't be so dramatic··· chill out A-Dawg.

I can chill, but you get the point right?

Read the guide 2-3 times
Use the guide
WHAM! You're in the money!

Homework

- :-) You know what to do··· Be positive and JUST DO IT!

Module 11: Where to Start???

Take these action steps to get a kickstart

1) Buy a domain at godaddy.com
2) Install the script you bought via videos
3) Build the site
4) visit http://www.warriorforum.com/warrior-joint-ventures/ and write a post saying this:

Title:

Massive Mini JV Giveaway Event coming up!

Message:

Are you looking for a bunch of new, fresh subscribers to add to your list? Wanna beat your best marketing buddy on the leaderboards? Wanna make some easy extra money? Got a quality free product to give away?

Good!

Make a squeeze page giving away the free product, and join HERE (you'll add your link here). Invite your best marketing buddy to see if you can beat him with signups / leaderboard status. We also have products for sale as well and you can make up to 50% on all sales.

Remember Join HERE, because start March 1st, 2015 this massive JV Giveaway Event will be rollin'!

Date and Time

If you use your own script··· allow 5-7 days to get all the contributors you can, then allow 14 days for the event.

Homework

- Understand this module and how things work
- FOLLOW ALL STEPS
- Move onto the next module

Module 12: Conclusion

Thank you, and Thank you, and Thank you yet again··· oh yeah and Thank you for buying and reading this product. I hope you had as much fun reading is as I did writing it.

If you use it, you'll go far, if you don't··· well I got nothin' for ya.

There is a lot more to learn, but most of that **_comes from ACTION_. You need to learn from yourself now that I've taught you about Making money from a freebie list and squeezing those profits!**

We went over:

- **How Mini JV Giveaway Events Work**
- **The Tools you'll need**
- **How to Easily set it all up and Find Contributors**
- **How to send traffic and also monetize your incoming traffic**
- **Sticking Points on where you may get stuck and how to solve them**
- **The amazing potential and outcomes if you decide to act!**

Please··· If nothing else, read this. Don't waste time, get out there NOW and get moving. Life isn't about circumstances, circumstances are excuses for us not to do something. Ask her out NOW, go to the gym NOW, start working NOW.

Got it?

Where will you be if you don't take action? Back right where you are in a year from now like I did for YEARS making up excuses. Don't do that. Take action, and thank you.

Homework

- Thank you!
- Be thankful!

How to contact me

You can find me on Facebook if you need to contact me or at my email address below. I'm online all the time, as it is my primary business.

Thank you!

Thanks for reading, and I will see you on the other side!

Aaron Autrey

support@aaronautrey.ru